Marvelous Messages From Your Faith

A Simple and Effective Method to
Manifest Your Desires and
Receive More Answers to Your Prayers

Jamie Linn Saloff

SENT
BOOKS

SENT BOOKS

Marvelous Messages from Your Faith.
Copyright © 2019, 2023, Jamie Linn Saloff. All rights reserved.

No part of this work may be reproduced in any manner whatsoever or otherwise be copied for public or private use, without written permission of the publisher, other than for "fair use" as brief quotations embodied in critical articles and reviews. Purchase only authorized electronic editions, and do not participate in or encourage electronic piracy of copyrighted materials. Your support of the author's rights is appreciated. Requests for permissions should be addressed to:

Sent Books
P. O. Box 339
Edinboro, PA, 16412

Cover image, izumikobayashi/iStockPhoto.com, Plateresca/ iStockPhoto.com. Used with permission.

Print: ISBN 978-1-7325300-1-0
Ebook: ISBN 978-1-7325300-4-1
LCCN: 2019908505
First edition, © 2007, Revised edition © 2019, 2023 v. 2.06
Copyright information available upon request.

In memory of
Duane Barnes

Because, as he often reminded me,
not everyone has the Internet.

Visit Jamie's website at:
https://www.MarvelousMessages.com

Contents

All Prayers Are Heard 1

God Answers My Prayers; He Will Answer Yours Too 3

Let God Provide the Answer 7

Expect a Miracle 10

Moving Mountains. 17

Remember What Is Most Important 26

Nothing Is Ever Lost 31

Mouth Confession 34

Ask for the Desires of Your Heart 39

Visual Prayers for Healing. 43

Balancing the Energy Around You 45

Supercharging Your Food 48

Open Every Right Door. 53

When You Need a Sign 55

Praying for Your World 60

God's Little Surprises. 63

Next Steps 65

Last Thoughts	.67
About Jamie Saloff	.68
What Others Are Saying About Jamie	.70

All Prayers Are Heard

This book is non-denominational and can benefit anyone who prays or asks the universe for Divine help. I most often refer to the Divine as "God." Feel free to interpret "God" in whatever form you perceive the Divine (or Source).

At age five, I learned to pray to "God the Father" clasping my fingers together as if holding His hand. However, now that I am older, I no longer see God as a giant being sitting on a throne amid the clouds in heaven. Instead, I perceive "Him" more like an energy that surrounds us in all things and all ways, perhaps more like the Star Wars "Force." The Divine can be everywhere, in everything, accomplishing many an amazing thing—if we but believe. Because of my upbringing, I still pray to God and refer to the Divine as "He." Old habits die hard.

I believe God hears every prayer regardless of who you are, where you've been, or how your prayer is offered. He doesn't care if you say a prayer "right" or "wrong." He accepts each prayer with the same love and joy as a mother given a dandelion from her young son.

Beyond a shadow of a doubt, I know that no prayer is considered too big, too small, or unimportant to God. No prayer is too hard for God. It is only in our *belief* (or lack thereof) that the difficulty arises.

Sometimes when we pray—although unintentional—we get in God's way. We make it harder for His miracles to happen. It's not our fault. Very few of us have ever been taught *how* to pray.

In this book, I'll show you how to open your prayers to greater possibility. Regardless of your beliefs or how you worship or recognize the Divine, I'll explain how to increase your prayer success rate and make your prayers more effective.

The techniques shared are extremely simple and only require the use of several basic principles. Years ago, I wrote a series of e-mails entitled "The Prayer Report." From those simple thoughts, I published a book called *Prayer Superchargers,* which was dearly loved by all who owned it. This is an expanded and revised version of that book.

While I can't promise miracles for everyone, I know they occur every day. I've witnessed many miracles myself. I hope you'll give these Superchargers a try and that you too will manifest your heart's deepest desires have many answered prayers.

God Answers My Prayers; He Will Answer Yours Too

I have been praying nearly all my life. I'm not sure why I became such a prayer warrior as my parents stopped going to church when I was about three years old.

As my mother once explained it to me, they had pledged a tithe toward the building of a new church. Not long after, my father became severely ill and nearly died. Due to the extensive hospital bills and not working, his income suffered, preventing them from honoring the expected payment. In response to our family's time of need, the elders came to our home and excommunicated my parents from the church.

Despite this shocking event, God touched me early on. I first learned to pray in vacation bible school, (ironically, at the newly built church). I also began squirreling away trinkets of faith.

While visiting a friend, I noticed a small gold cross still in its box tossed aside in her playroom. Easter had recently come and gone. When I asked her why she hadn't opened it, said she didn't want it and gave it to me. (She asked her mother first.) I could tell it meant nothing to her and couldn't understand why. For me, it seemed precious and called out to me. Sometime later, I found a tiny prayer book on my mother's desk. I pilfered it and hid it with my other collected things. I still have them, even after more than fifty years.

Because my parents rarely spoke about religion, it caught me by surprise when my mother stuck a prayer book in my stocking one Christmas eve. The real surprise came when I realized the private prayers I offered aloud each night had been overheard. (In those days, I believed kneeling at my bedside and speaking aloud made it easier for God to hear me.)

At first, I felt embarrassed because my prayers were a personal conversation between myself and God. But the discovery also made me happy to know my parents received hope from hearing my prayers. My father had been ill off and on for many years. He had overcome many near-death situations—perhaps due to my prayers? I kept praying, just in case, but maybe a little quieter.

Later in life, I learned my great-grandfather had been a preacher. My mother's great grandfather, George Long, had donated land in 1851 to build the Siloam school/church in his cornfields near Salem, Illinois. From that gift came forth many family preachers and teachers, including my great-grandfather, Rev. Henry Long. Perhaps my faith trickled down from them.

Or maybe my mother transferred it to me through a miraculous power within her. She became seriously ill as a small child. Her mother took her by train to see a faith healer and she recovered. Regardless of its origins, I didn't notice how my prayers might differ from anyone else's—though it's not typically something we compare. And while I didn't really talk about it, others did take notice. Soon, family and others were asking me to "say a prayer" whenever an especially trying circumstance arose. I would remind them how their prayers were just as powerful as mine. They didn't always believe me because they didn't feel their prayers were being answered, or at least they hadn't noticed that they were.

My prayers are certainly not any more eloquent than anyone else's, nor are they spoken with any special words. In fact, I often find shorter is better than longer, and, yes, I usually talk to God like I'd speak to any normal person. It's not so much WHAT I say when I pray, but HOW I frame my prayers. The latter is what I hope to convey in this book.

*For my thoughts are not your thoughts,
neither are your ways my ways, saith the Lord.*

Isaiah 55:8, KJV

Let God Provide the Answer

One of the things I've always tried to do is let God provide the answer. Not giving God the power to supply the answer is one of the most common mistakes we all make when praying.

Too often, we tell God *how* to solve our problems. That makes it harder for Him to send an appropriate answer. While we are waiting around for *our* answer, many of His go unnoticed.

Just as we can't always give our children what they want—in the way they want it—God sometimes has a better idea.

Here is the first of my Superchargers, one you can begin using right away. Whenever you pray, don't try to figure out how to solve the problem. Let God come up with the answer. Your job is to tell God exactly what the problem is.

For example, if your car is broken down along the highway...

> *Don't pray for God to send a tow truck.*
>
> *Don't pray that a kind trucker will stop and offer help.*

Don't pray that the car will miraculously start.

All of these things are great solutions. But they are not *God's* solutions, they are *yours*. They are *you* trying to figure out how to solve the problem. But that's not your job.

Does that mean that none of these things will turn out to be the answer?

Only God knows! So leave it to Him to figure out.

So what should you do instead?

Pray the problem.

Praying the problem sounds simple, yet many of us do not tell God what the problem is. Instead, we tell Him what we want the answer to be. Even I have caught myself trying to "help" God. (I bet He laughs when I do that.)

> Pray: *"My car is broken down and I need transportation."*
>
> Pray: *"I am ill, help me get well."*
>
> Pray: *"I am hungry and can't afford to buy food."*
>
> Pray: *"My home was destroyed by a flood; I've lost everything and don't know what to do.*

People Problems

There's another place where I see people praying the solution instead of the problem. It's when they are praying for others. Too many times we try to "fix" others by praying what *we* believe they need.

> *"Lord, Peggy needs a husband!"*
>
> *"Please help Jason get that factory job."*
>
> *"God, Melinda really needs a bigger house."*
>
> *"Bless Nathan and Jill with a child!"*

Maybe they don't need "fixed" (except in your eyes). Maybe your "fix" is not God's fix. Maybe what you want for them isn't what they want for themselves. Peggy may like being single. Jason may be an artist. Melinda's small house may be perfect for her needs. Nathan and Jill may not be ready for children.

It's never a good idea to play God with other people's lives by asking Him to create what *you* think is best. Especially when it comes to others, *pray the problem*. Watch as God works miracles that benefit them in ways you might never expect.

Of course, someone in your life may *ask* you to pray for them. In that case, pray as if it were your own situation. Pray the *problem* and let God deliver the solution. Even if they tell you the solution they desire—*pray the problem*.

Expect a Miracle

When you last prayed, did you expect to have prayerful success? Maybe? (Maybe not?) Or did you pray hoping for an answer you didn't believe would come?

Guess what? That is the second most common mistake we make when offering a prayer.

I can't believe how many people say a prayer and then include statements like these:

> *"God, I know you will never do this..."*
>
> *"I doubt you are even listening..."*
>
> *(sigh) "God, you never answer my prayers..."*
>
> *"I know I don't deserve this..."*

How can you expect to receive a miracle if you don't BELIEVE miracles can happen?

It is said that Jesus only could do a few miracles in his hometown because the residents did not believe in their possibility.

Belief in what you are praying for is a very important aspect of your prayer.

Some years ago, Norman Vincent Peale appeared in a television commercial advertising his *Guideposts* magazine and said the phrase now familiar to many, "Expect a miracle, make miracles happen." Maybe you remember it.

Here's another quote, this one from Ramtha:

> "Immaculate faith happens in a moment.
>
> "Immaculate curing, healing, restoration happens in a moment.
>
> "And the reason it takes so long for most of you?
>
> "Because the road is paved with doubt and disbelief."[1]

Prayers are about *belief* and nothing more. That is why the man in the bible said to Jesus, "Help me in my unbelief"—he knew he needed to first BELIEVE in the miracle before it could occur.

Praying isn't about how long it takes God to do something.

Praying is about encouraging yourself to believe it can happen. God already knows he can do it. Do YOU know that God can do it?

---

[1]. From, *Ramtha: A Beginner's Guide to Creating Reality*, (You may have heard of Ramtha in the movie *What the Bleep Do We Know!?*)

I want to let you in on a secret about myself. Sometimes I pray the same prayer over and over for an hour or more. Sometimes I might pray all day. Does it take God all day to answer? No! Does it take that long for my prayer to get to Him? No! Why do I keep praying, then? I pray until –I– believe it.

All that being said, some answers can provide an instantaneous result. Some answers take time. If you're praying to lose fifty pounds, the answer as to *how* may arrive instantly, but it will take time to see the weight fall off. Praying for a broken leg could see an instant healing, but likely it will take time to fully heal.

The first Supercharger I gave you is to "pray the problem." Now I want you to add to that, "expect an answer."

Expect your prayer will be answered and in a way that is beneficial to all involved.

Thus, since you are allowing God to figure out how to provide the answer, then you also need to be open to and *expecting* an answer, whatever it might be.

And, since you don't know how the answer might occur, you will look at everything in your life differently. You will see many avenues as a possible answer.

Do you know what that means?

Your life is suddenly filled with countless possibilities! Why?

Because if you are not locked into any *one* answer, especially an answer you've contrived, then you are going to find a whole world of possible answers!

Here's another question: How will you know you've received an answer if you don't know what the answer is?

When the problem you've prayed for is solved, of course! The fun part will be waiting to see *how* God supplies the answer, and that can be amazing!

I previously used a broken-down car for an example. Maybe you will suddenly remember you have a toolbox in your trunk and will discover you're able to repair the car yourself. (It's amazing what you can do with some duct tape and a bobby pin.)

Maybe you will notice a farmhouse through the trees where you can ask the residents for help.

Maybe the car will start on its own without any repair at all. (I've actually had this last one happen, so you could too.)

When you expect an answer to be forthcoming—and you know it might come from any or every possibility, your mind will find not just one answer, but a multitude of answers.

You might have to choose from several different answers!

(And you wondered if your prayer would be answered at all?)

When Your Belief Falters

Here is another Supercharger that goes with the last: Whenever I'm praying for something and I'm having a hard time believing in its possibility, I pray this little prayer:

"God, please make a way where there is no way."

I have seen some tremendous miracles using this simple prayer because, just by praying it, I am helping my own unbelief. I am telling myself that something can happen I don't necessarily believe there is any way it can happen . . . and it usually does!

When I first began working as a young adult, I didn't like one of my bosses. I had a good job for a just-out-of-high-school girl. I didn't want to find a new one. I prayed the "make a way" prayer not knowing how God would find a solution for me. Who could imagine the boss, the soon-to-be owner of the company, might leave? Not me. But that's exactly what happened. I didn't ask for that answer, I just prayed the problem. The answer was more perfect than I could have imagined!

My husband had a similar thing happen. His manager could be a real pain. He was the type of fellow who would take credit for other people's ideas, have long lunches, and other annoying idiosyncrasies. He unexpectedly took a new job in another state.

One day the former manager called my husband (who now held his managerial position) and said, "I don't know why I am here." (I do.) Prayers can be answered in marvelous ways.

Remember that "all things work together for good."

We don't always recognize this at the time, especially if we are caught up in something that feels frustrating, horrible, tragic, or sad. Use these Superchargers when a problem strikes, but also look around for the good in all that befalls you. I've been heard to say more than once...

"This is the best-worst thing that ever happened to me."

Although we don't always recognize it at the time, sometimes bad things happen for a good reason. As they say, "Where you're at, is where you're supposed to be."

I also sometimes find that when a roadblock appears in my life it may be to protect or help me.

The bible tells the story of Balaam's donkey who turned away from the path to avert Balaam's death. Balaam could not see an angel with a drawn sword ready to kill him, but the donkey did. Balaam tried to solve his problem by beating his donkey as he didn't see or understand what could be blocking his way.

After I have prayed for the problem, I also look around to discern what I may not be seeing that I should.

Remember that—you should *expect* answers. Make room in your belief for the unexpected. Keep an open mind and watch for the miracles that occur when you give them space to happen.

And Jesus said unto them...
If ye have faith as a grain of mustard seed,
ye shall say unto this mountain,
Remove hence to yonder place;
and it shall remove;
and nothing shall be impossible unto you.

Matthew 17:20 KJV

Moving Mountains

When Jesus says that we can move mountains, I'm pretty sure he meant . . . really . . . mountains . . . like those attached to the ground and mightily touching the sky. He wanted to show the truly immense power of prayer.

Have you ever seen anyone or even heard of anyone who has done that lately? I mean, without the use of tons of dynamite and heavy equipment? *(Me either.)*

Do you want to know why?

I want to make a small confession. When I first learned about moving mountains, I believed it so wholeheartedly that I would walk up to a wall, place my hand on it, and try to move my hand through it with prayer. I believed that if I did this properly, my hand would pass through the wall.

Can you guess what happened?

from Your Faith | 17

If you said nothing, you're right. So far, I have not been able to put my hand through any walls using the power of prayer.

Of course, that didn't stop me. I kept trying and trying. I tried tables too. I figured I just needed to do it longer or harder. I would sit and concentrate attempting to will my hand through the table. (Maybe I had seen too many science-fiction, superhero movies.) Still, nothing happened.

In the movie, *The Matrix*, a child bends spoons and says,

> *"Do not try and bend the spoon, that's impossible. Instead, only try to realize the truth. . . there is no spoon. Then you'll see that it is not the spoon that bends, it is only yourself."*

It sounds so easy. But it isn't, is it? Not when you are crying out desperately for your mountains to move, and they aren't.

If I can pray for or about anything, why can't I move mountains? Why is it that I cannot walk through walls or put my hand through a table? Why can't I eradicate illness, poverty, war, or death?

My father-in-law believed we would one day be able to regrow limbs. Why *can't* we regrow limbs? (Spiders do.) My father lost a leg, but the best he could do was replace it with a prosthesis. Yet, with the advent of stem cell therapies and new DNA discoveries, who knows what is possible in the future, *if we only believe. . .* These mountains *could* move!

You may have heard of the great Tibetan yogi, Milarepa, who believed in becoming one with his surroundings. In doing so, he left his handprints embedded in a Tibetan cave wall. The prints remain there to this day for others to see and touch. (So it *must* be possible?!)

But it hasn't been for me, and probably not for you. *Why not?*

I am sure there is a convoluted, scientific answer to this question, but I'm going to offer a simpler one. I am going to give you an answer that will enable you to transform your life.

Even though I thought that putting my hand through a solid wall was an interesting and intriguing idea, I didn't really expect it to happen because way deep down inside, I didn't honestly believe it *could* happen.

You've got to *believe*—that is paramount.

Unfortunately, I have lived too long in a world where everyone believes walls are solid and tables are too. We have learned to accept many of the atrocities in the world. There are some things we just don't know how to believe (or unbelieve).

Does that mean they can't happen?

Perhaps you have seen the old Peter Sellers movie, *Being There* where at the end, he walks on water. Do you know why he could? No one ever told him he couldn't!

from Your Faith | 19

I know, I know, that was just a movie with trick photography, but the point is still valid. Yet there are countless, documented cases of people who...

- died and came back to life
- miraculously recovered from terminal illness
- experienced other unbelievable feats and miracles.

Still, we find these things hard to believe in our own lives, even though we desperately want them.

This is what has happened in regards to our perception about walls, tables, mountains, spoons, **and difficult life situations**. We have never been taught that these things *could* be changed. So we don't know how to believe that they can. Instead, we've been taught that we must accept them as they are.

And, as I'm sure you've experienced—just saying, hoping, praying, trying to pretend you believe that you can move that mountain in your life—doesn't work. There is something deeper within us blocking our belief, perhaps on the subconscious level.

In order to believe the unbelievable, you've got to accept its possibility all the way down into the deepest of your core.

In one of my favorite movies, *Somewhere in Time*, Christopher Reeve utilizes everything in his surroundings to change his belief so he can go back in time. He cannot allow even one inkling of the present to enter his thoughts in order to succeed.

Sometimes mountains do move. Miracles do occur. Praying with fervent belief can shake the gates of heaven and change a difficult circumstance. While facing Hodgkins my father-in-law came to my bedside and said, "I saw a vision of the casket being put away." He prayed in faith to save my life (and I am still here).

In my previous chapters, I wrote how prayer is a means to help us believe. I wrote that when you can't believe something, to start by asking God to "Make a way where there is no way." Then I asked you to allow God to find the answer and to expect a beneficial answer.

Do you remember when I said, "How will you know when God has answered?"

"When the problem has been solved!"

But what about the really difficult problems?

What about the mountains in your life that need moving?

What about those "impossible" things? You know what I mean. I think we all have had mountain like that in our life:

- Someone you love is severely ill or has died . . .
- Your home has been destroyed . . .
- You're facing a life or death health crisis . . .
- Your child is missing . . .

from Your Faith | 21

When God Says No

Even though the impossible can be possible, sometimes it isn't. An old Garth Brooks song talks about *Unanswered Prayers*.

I know that some of you are really hurting. You pray, desperately seeking your answer. You long to know how to move mountains.

I am about to tell you there is another way, but it may not be the way you want to hear. This is going to be really hard to say. I am almost to tears as I write this because when we look at an impossible problem and we don't see "the mountain move," it is probably because we are still thinking that the answer to the problem is OUR answer. We wish that . . .

- ▷ Whoever died, didn't.
- ▷ Whatever tragedy happened, didn't.
- ▷ Whatever injustice occurred, didn't.

I know there have been times I wanted answers like that.

I hope you can hang on with me just one minute more because what I'm going to say is going to break down walls in your life and create a new possibility.

I know that there are those of you who are saying,

- ▷ *"My child is dying of cancer."*

- *"My wife was in a car wreck and is in a coma."*
- *"My house was flooded and I lost everything."*
- *"I'm totally bankrupt."*

And I know the answer you want because I would want that answer too. But those are *your* answers to the problem, and God is the problem-solving guy.

I have lost 14 significant relatives. I know what loss feels like.

I have had cancer—twice. I've looked in Death's face multiple times. I know what it feels like to be ill.

Not all my mountains moved (in the way I wanted). And this is what I learned from that—sometimes God knows better.

If I did not see the answer, I somehow didn't realize what God's answer was (and it would have been something beneficial).

We see our problems as if they are under a microscope. We don't always see the long-term, big picture. God does.

If I missed finding the answer, I might have also misdiagnosed the problem. We don't always clearly see what the real problem is amid a crisis. Additionally, we don't always see what the real solution can mean to our lives.

It is often the adversity we face that creates who we become and who we were meant to be.

Adversity is often the catalyst for something wonderful and special. (A hidden blessing.) It often offers a new life perspective.

Adversity can be something that severely affects one person or a group of people that, in turn, creates change in the lives of many.

Adversity can lead to:

- changes in our laws
- the creation of new, helpful organizations
- the bringing together of people or nations
- changes in our culture
- a needed change in perception or inspiration

During the Women's Suffrage Movement, thousands of women were ridiculed, beaten, and/or jailed while fighting for the right to vote. Thanks to their long-suffering determination, women in the U.S. obtained this right.

The death of Adam Walsch spurred his father, John, to create an organization and program to help find missing children.

Candace Lightner formed Mothers Against Drunk Driving, or MADD, after the death of her thirteen-year-old daughter, Cari.

These are the kinds of answers that occur around the difficult mountains we need to move. God's answer is to change our adversity into something good.

If you recently faced a mountain in your life, then this will be especially hard for you to see right now. You may still be suffering from grief, pain, stress, or hardship.

I know there are situations in your life that you will say, "What good came from *that*?!" My sister was hit by a car and killed. What good could come from that? Because of that, my mother deeply desired another child, and even though the doctors advised against it, she had me. My father passed of a horrible illness when I was just fifteen. What good could come from that? His trials led me to seek alternative paths of healing and to write about them. When my mother remarried, I learned things from my step-father I would have never learned from my father.

It's okay to give yourself time to grieve, to heal, and to ponder whenever life situations befall you. But keep looking for the good that is to come. If you allow it, the answer God sees and has sent will come. Mountains do move, just not always in the way we expect.

Here is a prayer to say in difficult situations.

> *Lord, God, please help me in this difficult situation of _____. Guide me in understanding how to make this mountain move. Strengthen my belief and show me the way where I see no way. Allow me to see the blessings from this and to know I'm being guided through it. Touch me with a peace that surpasses all understanding and walk with me through this trial day by day.*

Remember What Is Most Important

Would you like to learn how to turn a situation to good, even if appears to be going all wrong?

Here's one example of how that happened to me. It might seem trivial compared to some of the situations you find yourself in, but prayer works in any type of situation when you use the Superchargers I have shared.

My husband purchased concert tickets for a band we'd been wanting to see for years. We were so excited. We arranged to meet some friends beforehand for dinner and intended to then travel together to the venue. We'd been told we would need to arrive early since we had general admission tickets to a standing-room-only event and expected to be waiting quite a while outside on a cold and blustery winter's eve.

We waited for our friends at the restaurant, but an hour after the time we were to meet, they still hadn't arrived. The large establishment had quickly filled on a busy night. At last, giving up on our friends ever coming, we stood to leave. That's when they walked in.

We sat down and immediately ordered food since our time had shortened. While awaiting our food, we enjoyed each others company. I guess we lost track of time. All at once, we realized our meals had never come and we needed to get going if we were going to have seats. We'd now be much farther back in line.

What happened next was utterly amazing.

I began to pray silently, but I wanted to keep in mind what was really important for the day:

- We didn't want to miss any of the concert.
- We wanted a good meal.
- We wanted to enjoy the evening.

You might also think of it as, I prayed the problem:

- Our food hasn't come
- We don't want to miss the concert
- We want to have an enjoyable time without stress

I may have secretly added:

- We would like to have good seats
- We do not want to be stuck in the freezing cold

from Your Faith

As I prayed, I began to look around for our waitress, who we hadn't seen in a while. I noticed her across the room, pouring soft drinks for another table. As I finished my prayer, I noticed that she appeared startled by something, nearly knocking over the drink cup she had been filling. (Perhaps an angel tapped her on the shoulder?) Just as suddenly, she turned and ran out of the room toward the kitchen. (Had it worked?)

Directly after, the manager came over to our table and said our order had been lost. He apologized profusely, saying he would give us our meal *without charge* and that they were doing all they could to get our food to us right away. And they did.

But the incredible turn of events did not stop there. In fact, they got even better!

We ate as quickly as we could, knowing we were running much later than expected. We did not know if we would have seats or be able to see the band at all. To make matters worse, the friend's wife had just revealed she was pregnant! We didn't want to cause her any duress.

As we walked up to the hall we found no line. Most of the people were already inside. Walking through the door, we were greeted by a saleswoman from a cell phone company.

Apparently, she'd been sent to promote their new cell phones, but people were so rushed to ensure they had seats, no one would talk to her. She seemed desperate to talk to anyone, so I asked her what it was all about. She asked us a couple of quick questions and then handed us passes to a posh, private seating VIP room to thank us.

We were escorted to the room as if we were royalty. We were served drinks and waited comfortably until the concert began. Better still, we had a sneak peek at the band who were eating their dinner in the adjoining room.

Because of our access to this exclusive room, we had entry to a private balcony area where we had front row seating. We could not have asked for better sightlines or more comfortable seats. We immensely enjoyed the concert as well.

This sure beat standing out in the cold for an hour!

After this turn of events, I kept thinking of how the night might have turned out if I hadn't prayed or had lost track of what was most important for the night.

- If we had left early, we wouldn't have met up with our friends.

- If we had become angry at the restaurant, we might not have eaten such good food, and without charge.

- If we had worried about the time, we might have left our food, which was delicious, despite the delay.

- If we had rushed to the concert hall to stand in line, we might have been a blur among the crowd and likely would not have been chosen for the special passes ... and it would have been cold!

All of what happened turned for good because we kept our focus on what was most important. My prayer received a wondrous reply, one more marvelous than any I could have ever wished for.

Always keep in mind what is most important.

Nothing Is Ever Lost

My favorite, everyday watch had been missing for months. I had looked everywhere but hadn't found it. The watch had been gone for so long, most people would have given up. But I didn't. I felt I would still find it.

I had read somewhere that "nothing is ever lost" to God, that he always knows where everything is. So I began to pray that God would find my watch.

The watch wasn't very expensive. I could have easily bought a new one. I just always had liked it and wanted it back.

One day while out golfing, I started digging in my golf bag for something. For some reason, I opened a pocket I rarely opened.

Guess what was inside?

My watch! The battery had died, but otherwise, it was in perfect condition. I didn't even remember putting my watch in my golf bag. Finding my watch grew my faith, so I tried it on some other things.

from Your Faith

We had a sign hanging in front of our house, as many of the cottages in our lakeside neighborhood had names. One day it disappeared. We informed the police, but they did not offer us much hope of recovering it.

My husband wanted to make a new one, but I kept telling him no. I knew our sign would somehow find its way home. God knew where to find the sign, so I left it up to him.

A few months passed.

We were sitting on our front deck when a car stopped out front. A man called from his car, "Did you used to have a sign hanging here?" He pointed to the lamp post and empty hangers.

"Yes," we replied.

Soon we learned that some college kids had stolen many local signs as part of a fraternity stunt and left them in a rental house this man owned. He found all the signs behind the piano when the students moved out. He decided to return any he could.

The sign now hangs in front of our home in its rightful place.

If you have lost something, God knows where it is.

This Supercharger has worked for me for a great many things. There are still some things I'm missing, but I am being patient.

My mother used to make dolls for the Christmas tree.[1] She sold them all over the country and through stores like Marshall Fields and Frederick Nelson. Of course, the best set was hers because she had all the originals including the ones that never made it to market.

During every holiday season, we honor my mother by hanging the ornaments she created on the tree. Unfortunately, my tree is a little bare. My mother always promised to give me her set since I didn't have one of my own. Sadly, due to complicated circumstances, they ended up with my stepfather's third wife, and, unbeknown to us, she sold them in a yard sale.

Some of my mother's ornaments have found their way home including a special one made just for me. In the sixth grade, I wrote a report on Finland. My mother made me a traditional Finnish dress to wear and a doll to match. I surely was blessed to find the doll, along with other of her ornaments on eBay.

Some are still out there, including her trademark piece, *The Storyteller* (an old man sitting in a rocking chair, slippered feet on a footstool, reading a book). God knows where to find *The Storyteller* and the other missing dolls. Someday, He will bring them home too.

If you've lost something you loved, God knows where it is. Ask him to find it for you, to protect it, and to bring it home safely.

---

[1]. If you'd like to see some of my mother's handmade creations, you can look on the website: www.iaulandas.com.

Mouth Confession

In our quest to find answers to our life's problems, we tend to grumble a bit along the way. I find in our daily conversations we have a tendency to:

- Poke fun at ourselves
- Take the blame for things we shouldn't
- Apologize for things that need no apology *(women especially do this)*
- Criticize, degrade, and belittle ourselves
- Become self-conscious if complimented

And, if someone doesn't, we may think that they are arrogant, headstrong, self-important, or a bitch.

When as a society did we begin to feel we didn't deserve good things? When did we decide it was better to be the least worthy person in the room? Why are we so uncomfortable about being who we are, what we wear, how we act, and what we do?

So, instead, we end up saying statements like:

- *I'm so dumb that I . . .*
- *Knowing my bad luck, I'll . . .*
- *I will never be that (rich, thin, smart, lucky).*
- *I could never do that.*
- *They would never choose me for . . .*
- *This old thing?*
- *If my head wasn't attached I'd lose it.*

In my book, *Hatch – A Change Your Life Guide*, I compare this kind of talk to walking around with one of those old-fashioned, plastic fly swatters. Each time you make a statement such as these, it's like you're whacking yourself with the swatter. *(Ouch!)*

STOP IT!

My father-in-law used to catch us saying these types of things. He'd remind us by simply saying, *"mouth confession."* Because he constantly pointed it out, I learned not to do it. (Mostly.)

By continually repeating some of the downgrading statements that we say over and over again to ourselves and others, we are drawing that energy and/or situation into our lives. Soon, we start believing them.

Some friends of ours used to joke how their home *"must have been built on an old burial ground"* because they had so much go wrong while living there. Of course, they repeated this often.

By mouth confession they convinced themselves that nothing could go right; no one could be trusted to do a job, products couldn't work without breaking, in general, they had bad luck. What they said is what they got, over and over again.

While *"mouth confession"* isn't exactly a prayer, it does play a vital role in what we ask for, how we ask for it, and our belief as to if it will come to pass. It also plays a role in our expectations.

"Deservability"

Receiving an answer to prayer isn't based on your "deservability." Answers to prayers come from belief, forward action, and the openness to possibility. It really doesn't matter how worthy you are, how "good" you've been, or how religious you appear to be. It simply comes down to asking for help in a situation where you feel helpless and believing that the help or guidance will arrive.

If you are belittling yourself—stop! You are here for a reason—a valid, important reason. You may or may not know what that reason is, but know that only you can be *you*.

Stop tearing yourself down. I'm betting you aren't all those nasty, hurtful, stupid, foolish, things you keep saying about yourself. Stop swatting yourself with that invisible swatter!

When you catch yourself confessing in a negative way, stop yourself—mid-sentence, if you can. Reimagine the negative in a positive light. If you turn your *"confessions"* around, you may find your prayerful results turn around as well.

Two of my favorite books on this topic are:

The Game of Life and How to Play It, by Florence Scovel Shinn and *Excuse Me, Your Life Is Waiting,* by Lynn Grabhorn. Shinn's work goes back to the 1800s and has been useful teaching for a long time. When I attended Fellowships in Lily Dale, NY, they incorporated Shinn's work into our teachings. I read the Grabhorn book nearly two decades ago at a time when I really needed to hear it, and it continues to be readily at hand on my bookshelf today.

To Supercharge your prayers, remember to:

Be conscious of what you confess. Always focus on positive, uplifting outcomes.

*Delight thyself also in the Lord:
and he shall give thee
the desires of thine heart.*

Psalms 37:4, KJV

Ask for the Desires of Your Heart

I love cars! Many years ago, I fell in love with Toyota's American-built, Chevrolet Nova. I saw one on the street in slate gray and wanted one so much. (Maybe I should have wanted a BMW or a Mercedes, but I only had a little faith, so I wanted a Nova. Even that felt like a huge, unobtainable goal at the time.)

I knew we couldn't afford it, so, instead, I just imagined what it would be like to have one. I told God I wanted that slate gray color and, oh, yeah, it had to have air conditioning, a stereo, and good pick-up (because my current ride struggled up our local hills as if it had a lame-legged, blind horse for a motor.)

I didn't tell anyone. I knew I should be happy with the car I had. (I had once asked for it too.) I didn't want to add to our already stretched budget. I didn't dwell on it and quickly forgot about it.

A few months later, my stepfather asked me to come see his new car. To my shock, sitting in his garage was MY dream car. No, he had no plans to give it to me. He didn't even know I wanted one. Yet, there sat my car down to every detail of my desire.

You can't imagine how it surprised me to see that car parked there. I reasoned it couldn't just be a coincidence. As long as I'd known him, my stepfather had only owned huge Cadillacs bought from his favorite Cadillac dealer. For him to have that little car did not even make sense!

Since I knew to allow God to find the solution, I surmised that someday the Toyota would be mine. I just didn't know how God would work it out.

I figured since God had put the car in my path, ***I needed to take some action*** to make that car mine. My stepfather and mother would soon be moving to Florida and planned to sell the car at that time. I wanted to offer to buy it, but couldn't afford it, so instead, I offered to sell it for them when they moved.

Eventually, the car came some 90 miles away to our house, and for a few weeks, it sat in our yard with a for sale sign on it. Even though we lived on a busy state route where we had sold several cars in just a couple of days, *no one* stopped to look at the car.

(I had considered parking the car in the garage while my husband was at work each day so no one would know it was for sale, but I didn't.) Again, I felt as though the car was to be mine, but how?

By now, my husband knew I wanted it, but how could we afford it? With two small, fast-growing boys, our dollars went fast. And talk about "deservability," well in those days I often went without so my family could have their needs fulfilled. I would not have counted myself worthy of such a gift in those days.

However, apparently, my husband did. He bought me that car when he unexpectedly received a bonus that "coincidentally" equaled the price my stepfather was asking for the car. (I should mention that I don't believe in "coincidences.")

When my husband told me I could have the car, my heart leapt with joy. I can't tell you how happy it made me to own that car. I drove it for many years and still think of it fondly.

You can Supercharger your desires when you allow yourself to clearly define the details. Draw pictures, cut out photos. I find it especially helpful if I can employ my other senses, such as smell, hearing, or any accompanied feelings. I can't tell you how many cars (and other things) I received in this way. Some call this "Law of Attraction," but I only knew it as prayer in those days.

And remember how I couldn't think big enough for a Mercedes? Well, one day I fell in love with a Lincoln. Not just any Lincoln, but a Navigator. That car was so big the first dealer suggested I buy a little car instead! (Never tell a lady the car is too big for her! We bought it elsewhere!) Many other cars followed.

However, my Toyota FJ may be my most favorite vehicle of all. How I came to get that one still amazes me. Long since having gotten over "deservability" and small goals, a Lexus caught my eye. I even lingered over one at a car show, despite my husband's protests. But the Lexus *was* a little out of the range of our needs and what we wanted to spend. It left me in a dilemma. I sat down to figure out what I really wanted.

- A Lexus? (Well, maybe not.)
- Something that looked different. I didn't want a car that looked like a benign box. It had to be fun.
- Good pick-up and great in snow. (We get a lot of snow. I mean a lot.)
- Affordability. Versatility. Reliability.

Just before Christmas, my husband showed me a picture of the then, newly-re-released, Toyoto FJs. "What *is* that?!" I asked. The FJ did not look like *anything* I had ever seen. (I didn't know Toyota had revamped a previously made vehicle.) Soon, I had a Voodoo Blue Toyota FJ in my driveway. And the most surprising thing of all? Some of the underpinnings are taken from Lexus. (And you thought God didn't listen to prayers?)

Remember that it is your job to have the desire and God's job to find a way to make it happen.

- If God opens a door of opportunity, even if you are unsure how it will work out, walk through it. Your desire may be just on the other side.
- Do not try to force what you want into being. Patience and trust must come into play.
- Believe and Expect that God will find a way.
- Say THANK YOU and share your joy with others when it finally arrives. (This is an important step.)

Visual Prayers for Healing

I'm lucky in that when I received my Hodkins diagnosis in the 1980s, concepts like healing visualization were becoming more mainstream. Late one night in the hospital, I switched on my TV just as a documentary about Dr. Bernie Siegel aired. Siegel had been experimenting with cancer patients, including visualization as part of their treatment. Intrigued, I started thinking of mini *Ghostbusters* (a newly released movie at that time) maneuvering through my bloodstream, zapping all the cancer cells.

While visualization wasn't the only method I self-employed, it did begin to change my views about healing. (I also endured the prescribed medical treatments and surgeries.) Like Siegel, Lousie Hay, and others, I started to acknowledge that illness often had an emotional connection at its core, though it would be many more years before I could put that into words and create my own system for unveiling them.

By the time I received my breast cancer diagnosis some thirty years later (said likely to be due to a side effect from the previous medical treatments), a whole wide world of alternative therapies and view points had come to light.

As I often laid awake late at night during my chemotherapy, I would visualize healing for myself. Some of the methods I used included:

- Seeing myself on a table in a sterile room where above me hung multi-colored lights. I could see this light entering my body and healing it. (I initially saw this in a dream, but later learned there were actually places where this was done.)

- Visualizing "sparkling golden goo" flowing down into and throughout my whole body healing it. (This from a teaching taught by the late, Reverend Shirley Caulkins Smith.

- I would visualize my tumor getting smaller and falling off (which it eventually did).

I'm sure I used my vivid imagination in countless other ways while nearly eight months of treatments and surgeries passed by.

Like other forms of prayer, visualization requires belief. Yet, at the same time, visualization can be a means of boosting a waining belief. I find visualization doesn't have to be perfect, continual, or overly diligent. In fact, it can often simply be fun.

Supercharge your healing prayers; add in some visualization.

Balancing the Energy Around You

There have been many times I needed a quick, effective prayer. Sometimes, I only have time to whisper a quick word under my breath or, maybe, I want to remain discrete.

Friend and author, Joey Korn, taught me the following prayer. (You can learn more about his prayers at www.dowsers.com.) I have found it useful in countless situations, filling in the blank with any appropriate statement:

> *Dear God, create a unique energy configuration specific to this need by balancing any detrimental energies and enhancing any beneficial energies in order that ____.*
> *For now and for as long as it is appropriate, Amen.*

▷ For noisy restaurants:

> *...the area surrounding us might be filled with peace.*

▷ While driving on icy and snow-covered roads:

> *...we are able to drive home safely.*

- During an argument:

    ...we might find a calm resolution.

- Or to keep volatile attitudes from entering my home:

    ... only love may enter this abode.

- Flying in an airplane:

    ...the plane might have safe skies so we arrive safely.

I've used this prayer in many ways, many, many times. It's often my first go-to prayer in a situation. It works best when I say the prayer silently to myself and release it. I tend to forget about it only to realize, perhaps twenty minutes later, it's come to pass.

When a Storm Is Threatening

As a small child, I remember staring out our sliding-glass doors trembling in fear of a coming storm. Any severe thunderstorm hijacked my senses and caused me much fear. My parents had become used to my anxiety over this but tried to pass it off as silly until, on this day, my mother confessed her blame.

I was born early in 1960 when American suburbanites were still building fallout shelters in case of nuclear war. While still a babe in the cradle, a huge clap of thunder hit in the dark of night. My mother, fearing "the bomb," rushed into my bedroom, grabbed me from my crib, and covered me with her body on the floor. I'm not sure how long she laid there before she realized a bomb hadn't dropped but rain had come. After learning this, I found it easier to face my fear.

Decades later, I can still sense, perhaps due to certain barometric pressures, when a storm is more threatening than a common downpour. I tend to pace, and, of course, pray, until the danger of the storm has passed.

I often use the balancing prayer for storms including potential hurricanes, tornadoes, and other threatening weather. Although I don't always see abatement of the storm, I often wonder if it could have been worse had I not prayed.

> *Dear God, create a unique energy configuration balancing any detrimental energies and enhancing any beneficial energies to protect my home from damaging wind, rain, hail, and other acts of nature. Protect my family, pets, and possessions. Protect my neighbors, and those around me. Protect my town. For now and for as long as it is appropriate, Amen.*

When praying for a specific storm, I might pray:

> *Dear God, create a unique energy configuration balancing any detrimental energies and enhancing any beneficial energies to calm the winds of _____ (hurricane's name). Calm its winds, push it away from land, and disperse its fury.*

Supercharging Your Food

I grew up in a home that didn't say grace at meals. I knew others did. It wasn't anything I gave much thought to. As I mentioned previously, we didn't talk much about God or religion at home.

Just before my nineteenth birthday, my mother remarried. My mother sold our family home, so I went to live with them for a few months prior to my own marriage.

Being a devout Catholic, my stepfather, John, attended church every morning before work and said grace at every meal. While I politely lowered my head and waited, the rote words he quickly rattled off did not feel very important to me.

On the contrary, my soon-to-be in-laws would offer a from-the-heart prayer incorporating any pressing needs of the day. Their words seemed to offer more meaning to those at the table. Even then, I didn't consider the food and the prayers as connected. Grateful for the food, yes. Empowering the food, no. I thought of the meal's blessing more of a ritual rather than anything that might be beneficial to the food in front of me.

During my spiritual training, I experienced something amazing that changed my viewpoint on prayers for food.

We were taught by many mentors. One of them, Tom Cratsley, a gifted healer, guided us in learning about green pepper healings. He explained how he would ask the peppers to assist us in the ceremony and that the peppers would draw out toxins from the participant's body. I volunteered to sit for the demonstration.

Before beginning, he asked what I would like cleared. Having received radiation therapy and many drugs and chemicals in my past due to cancer, I requested clearing any remaining residues that might still remain from that.

The class sat around me in a semicircle while he prayed over the peppers. He asked the peppers for their assistance and blessing, then cut them in half. He held them a few inches from my body, praying, and giving them time to do whatever the peppers were supposed to do.

It didn't take long until many of us smelled an odd, unpleasant odor. Truly, the peppers appeared to be extracting something from me (or somewhere) and collecting it within themselves. Afterward, I felt lighter and happier, but unsure of what had really happened.

I can't explain what occurred during the healing and can't prove that any toxins actually left my body. I don't know what caused the smell we noticed. As students, we were given the opportunity to try the process ourselves. Neither my partner nor myself had a similar experience. Even though we followed the protocols as closely as possible, we didn't smell anything odd and didn't feelnany physical differences. Yet, we all knew something amazing had taken place during my initial healing.

After that experience, I gained a new appreciation for the life force carried by plants. I can't say I immediately started praying over my food or that I regularly talk to my produce. But what happened on that day stayed with me.

Sometime later, a friend explained how the blessings we put into food begin as we prepare it. When we carefully wash, trim, and season our food, even as we stir and simmer it, we are putting our love into the whole meal. As we sit down to eat and offer a blessing over our food, we are again imbuing the food with love and positive energies that can heal and enliven us.

This is quite different from mass produced, heavily fertilized fruits and vegetables that are chemically sanitized, run through a series of electric chopping machines, pureed, and overcooked beyond recognition for a frozen, boxed dinner.

While I don't regularly ask the living cells of my produce to partner in my quest for health and well being, it isn't as far fetched as it may seem. Scientific evidence shows plants do respond to conversation (though scientists disagree as to why).

Keep in mind, however, that any plants' ability to help may be hindered by the environment in which they were grown. Their ultimate cell structure and biological components could have been altered by substandard soil, toxic or poisonous substances put on them, or poor growing conditions.

Offering a prayer over your meal *can* be beneficial, not just in giving thanks for the meal about to be received, but in creating a blessing that enhances the food itself. You can pray over the food, asking it to carry with it properties of healing, well being, and other beneficial enhancements. This is, in essence, what Jesus did when he turned water into wine. (Talking to your produce is something I'll let you decide for yourself.)

> **Supercharge your food by offering a blessing over it before eating or serving it to others.**

*"Whether you turn to the right or to the left,
your ears will hear a voice behind you, saying,
'This is the way; walk in it.'"*

*Isaiah 30:21,
New International Version*

Open Every Right Door

We live in a world filled with many marvelous opportunities and possibilities. But, sometimes, we are faced with too many options and are unsure which one might be the "right" one.

Over the years I've come to believe we can't really make a wrong decision—provided we made the best choice we could with the information we had at the time. Later on, we may feel we could have chosen better, but we must recognize we couldn't see the whole picture at the time. It's always easy to judge our decisions in retrospect.

When I am faced with a choice that seems like either way might be equal in its pros and cons, and when I am really unsure what the right choice might be, I pray the following prayer:

Lord, God, open every right door and close every wrong door.

After I have prayed this prayer, I then sit back and wait to see what will transpire.

When my husband and I decided to go hunting for our first home, we looked at a landscaper's home. Though older, it had been well kept. I fell in love with the lush backyard and dearly loved that house. Unfortunately, they wanted more than we could afford and would not budge on their price.

I'd been taught to claim what I wanted, so I declared, "I am claiming that house as mine!" I believed God would find a way to make it ours. Occasionally, I'd drive by and see the "for sale" sign still in the yard. Again, I would claim it as ours.

At least a year went by, and honestly, I forgot about the house. Our situation changed. We found a lovely house, purchased it, and moved in. Sometime after that, I happened to notice the other house still on the market for sale. I realized that, even though I still loved the house and beautifully landscaped yard, the house we purchased better fit our needs. I suddenly felt bad and wondered if I'd caused the other house not to sell for all those months. (More than likely, they had just overpriced it for their market and continued to resist lowering their price.)

I prayed, releasing the house, asking God to sell it quickly. (And it soon did.) I realized after that to always pray, **"this or better"** whenever I "claimed" something I wanted.

The "right door" prayer Supercharger is great for home searches, job seeking, and other life-shaping decisions. Or sometimes you just want a "sign" …

When You Need a Sign

Have you ever asked God to send you a sign for what you should or should not do? Did you get a reply?

There are times when signs have a pre-set meaning.

- ▷ We always know my cousin Kerry is watching over us from above when we find dimes in odd places.

- ▷ Swans have always been very symbolic to me. I decided to extend my schooling when I found swans in the Lily Dale hotel wallpaper.

- ▷ Prior to a surgery that went awry, I ran into countless signs of phoenix birds, known to rise up from the ashes.

- ▷ One friend of mine finds feathers when she needs a sign, another sees dragonflies.

Sometimes we don't have a pre-set sign but desire guidance when making a decision.

from Your Faith

Many years ago, when our children were still very small, we set out to find our first family home. Every weekend, we piled the boys into the car and trolled through local neighborhoods looking for a house that fit both our budget and needs.

Eventually, we hooked up with a great Realtor (Karen) who recognized that we really didn't have a clue as to what we wanted in a home. She showed us a series of very different houses, and then, from our comments, was able to understand better what we liked and what we didn't.

As I walked inside each new house, I waited to be wooed and hoped for a sure knowing—*"This is the one!"* But that didn't happen.

I prayed for some sign . . . if only bells sounded, or whistles blew. I watched for any sign to let me know which house would be the right house for us. Still, nothing happened.

After our initial visits, Karen took us to the house that she was sure would be our favorite. We loved the wooded yard and circular drive. Inside, we found everything we could want in a home. I waited, still hoping for any sign, but received none.

Several weeks went by and we went to view yet another house. I looked through the rooms somewhat benignly because nothing about them particularly interested me. To be truthful, something about the house made me feel downright uncomfortable.

To my surprise, I overheard my husband and Karen talking about placing a bid. Before I could even think about my response, I blurted out, "But the other house was so much better!" They both looked at me with their mouths wide open. "Which 'other house'?" My husband and Karen waited for the answer without a clue.

"Why the one with the lovely wooded yard and circular drive, of course."

Well, a flurry of conversation ensued where we determined that neither of us had really shared with the other how we felt about that home. We each had assumed the other didn't like it due to it being further out of town.

Before I knew it, we were checking that home's availability. Yes, amazingly, it had remained on the market. We quickly placed our bid, which, as you might guess, they accepted.

I learned from that experience that sometimes the "sign" we are looking for is not in knowing the *right* answer as much as it is in knowing the *wrong* one.

I believe that there wasn't so much a "right" house for us, as many of the homes we looked at could have been a happy home. There were homes that were the "wrong" house for us. The other home sat on the corner of a busy street, not the right location for two small kids. So, by following the feelings inside me, we were able to find the perfect home for our family. My feelings were my "sign."

We had many happy years and memories in that home and then, eventually, we outgrew it. We once again went house looking. I once again waited for a sign.

This time, something different happened. We looked at a home set on a lake near a playground. We knew our boys would love it. Unfortunately, they had listed the house out of our price range, so we didn't bid.

A few weeks later, while the boys were at the same playground, we noticed another couple looking in the windows of the house. Again without thinking, I blurted, "Those people are looking in our windows! That's 'our' house!"

We contacted Karen once more and learned the price had been reduced. In a few weeks, we were its new owners. We've lived in that home for many years and plan to continue doing so for many more. My "sign" was the gut feeling I felt when I saw the other couple looking at the house.

When you need a sign, check your inner feelings.

When you hit the "wrong" button, you'll know it. Sometimes that's the only sign you'll need. Sometimes you'll just "feel" what is right or wrong.

Fast forward many years. Our sons grew up, were single and still living at home. We began looking for a little place where they could share the costs and move forward into their adult lives.

We looked at several little cottages in the area. I had my hopes on one situated behind our house across our back street. Our neighbor, a former Realtor, said, "it's a teardown," meaning she considered the house unlivable. We felt we could do the necessary work, so we bid on it. The owners countered our bid, we countered their counter, but then the negotiations stopped. They did not even bother to respond to our last offer. We were too far apart.

Undeterred, we continued shopping around and found a cute little cottage the owners had recently renovated. We were even able to purchase the furnishings, giving our sons a like-new home just a few blocks away from ours.

As the years have gone by, we've realized how fortunate we were to find their little house. Not long after our bid, they, indeed, did tear down the other. The lot sat vacant for eight years before it finally sold for far below what we had offered.

Even when something seems perfect, that doesn't mean that it is the "right" one. When we trust in faith and allow God to move freely, we can be led to what is truly the "right door."

Praying for Your World

Most of us live in a world where we are constantly barraged by the media and their messages of alarm. Radio, TV, newspapers, and the Internet all make sure we are reminded of the horrible terrors in the world including war, poverty, abuse, injustice, illness, and death. We are surely living in Pandora's box and must seek hope, faith, and love on our own if we really want to find it.

How should we pray for our world? How can we make it a better place to live? Can there ever be "peace on Earth," with "goodwill towards all men?"

I believe that our outer world is a reflection of our inner world. While there might be some blurring of the lines, when our focus tunes in to the wars of the world, it may be that we have a war going on within or around us—maybe not with guns and soldiers, bombs, and death, but a battle, nonetheless.

As my father lay upstairs in his bedroom suffering through his last days, I found my mother standing alone in the darkened family room holding a bible in her hand. Using the evening light coming in the sliding door, she had been reading. Startled by my presence, she tried to hide the book. Realizing the futility, she said only, "Every time I open it, I only find war."

She explained further that, whenever troubled, she would think of her problem and then randomly open the bible to wherever it fell. Truly, she was experiencing a war. A war to save my father's life or, at least, ease his constant pain; a war with the doctors who said they could do no more; a war with God, who she may have felt did not hear her pleas. While there were no guns blazing, no battle tanks, the battle raged on.

When my father died, my mother took care of all the necessary details, filings, payments, and letting go of things. Then she picked herself up by the bootstraps and did what she needed to do to heal her life from the internal war she'd been through. It took faith and determination for her to do that. She knew she needed to be her best so she could continue raising me and to be there for the rest of the family.

Blessed are those who are willing to stand up and advocate for change. Blessed are those who have fought and maybe even died for the rights we have today. Blessed are those who, when they could not give of themselves, gave of their hard-earned funds to support those who could.

But what can the rest of us do? We can pray and we can work on betterment of ourselves, our personal environment, and that which is in our personal world. That is what I saw my mother do. That is what I do as well.

I do pray for the world, When I do, I see light shining down from the heavens onto the globe that is our planet. I ask for the highest and best outcome. More than that, I strive to be a better person in my world. I strive to improve the world around me, starting with myself, my home, my family, and my neighbors.

When I walk down the street or through a store, I often see people making their way despite visible hardships. Maybe they have a limp. Maybe I've just overheard some sadness in their checkout conversation. Maybe they just look like they need a smile today. I've never been all that out-going. I'm not that person who just walks up to strangers and starts talking to them. But I can pray for them. I visualize sparkly light shining around them and ask God to bless them in some beneficial way.

I am not an activist. I thank God for those who are. I am not a humanitarian. I am grateful they are in the world to do the good they do. I am a writer. We each have our gifts and our place. Use what you have for good. The more of us who do, the better the world will be.

> **Pray for the world. Continually improve upon yourself. The world will be a better place for all.**

God's Little Surprises

In one of my favorite television episodes of *X-Files*, Mulder (David Duchovny) meets a jinni (a female genie) who enjoys playing games with people's wishes. Unfortunately, she gets her kicks twisting their wishes so the answer is not as expected.

When Mulder wishes for "peace on earth," he gets it. He finds himself alone amid empty cars and buildings of the city. In effect, he is the only one on earth. With no one else to make noise or war, there is peace—just not in the form he expected.

Mulder then takes to writing a contractual-like wish. He fills pages and pages with conditions, stipulations, and exceptions until he realizes even with all that it is useless. There is always some loophole. So instead, he uses his last wish to free the jinni.

The potential of these odd little twists in our prayers reminds us that we are playing with a tremendous power that we do not fully understand, a power that can, indeed, alter our lives. I think the twists are a warning and a reminder to use that power with care.

So pray without ceasing. Ask for all your heart's desires. But do be mindful of what you pray for—you might just get it.

*"Don't focus on how big your problem is,
be amazed at how gigantic your God is."*

Teresa Shields Parker

Next Steps

Marvelous Messages from Your Faith is part of the Connection Level of the Marvelous Messages process. Other levels include the Heart (your deepest desires), Root (your heritage), Overcoming Obstacles (blocking your way), and Transformation (ascension) — or more precisely, achieving that "happy place" you've sought for so long.

I recommend you explore the Heart level first, as this will lead you to all else you desire. The Heart level books include *Marvelous Messages from Your Body*, *Marvelous Messages from Your Childhood*, and my forthcoming book, *Marvelous Messages from Your Heart*.

Next, I recommend exploring your roots, as you will uncover some of the innate challenges ingrained within you and the means to overcome them. I explain this in my book, *Hatch – A Change Your Life Guide,* or watch for my forthcoming book *Marvelous Messages from Your Ancestry* and its accompanying card deck for more hands-on guidance.

In private coaching with me, we work together through this process to reveal your innate challenges and free your most heartfelt desires. I use my intuitive abilities to part the veil and connect with your ancestry. We explore your challenges, desires, and their core essence on multiple levels. Visit my website to learn more.

In addition, you might consider any of the following options:

- ▷ Watch for additional *Marvelous Messages* books coming soon.
- ▷ Visit my website for additional articles, audios, videos, resource links, and other materials designed to help you utilize your Marvelous Messages.
- ▷ Watch for my interactive classes and coaching.
- ▷ Check for my Facebook groups and connect with me via social media.

If you're ready to experience more, visit my website at:

www.MarvelousMessages.com

Last Thoughts

Can I ask a favor? If you enjoyed *Marvelous Messages from Your Faith* it would mean a lot if you would let your friends know so they can also experience these enlightening thoughts and mind-opening ideas. Most book reading platforms make it easy to click and share.

If you leave a review for the book on the site from which you purchased it, on Goodreads, your own blog, or your favorite social media platform, I would love to read it. Email me the link at **info@saloff.com**.

I would also enjoy hearing about your experiences using any part of my Marvelous Messages™ process. Email me or feel free to post your questions and comments on my website or any of my social media platforms (links are in my bio at the end of the book). Your valuable feedback helps me to evolve my systems so they can better help others.

About Jamie Linn Saloff

Author, teacher, story weaver, spiritual counselor, seer of visions, pathfinder. . . for over thirty years Jamie has taught type-A-driven free spirits how to become happy, healthy, and wealthy by listening to their body groan and their soul weep.

Jamie strongly believes in the inherent power of our ancestry and in *"looking back to leap forward."* She has frequently appeared as a radio personality, guest blogger, and workshop leader. She has written and been featured in countless articles, blogs, newsletters, and newspapers. Jamie has authored twelve books including:

- *Hatch – A Change Your Life Guide*

- *Marvelous Messages from Your Body: Learn the Meaning of an Ailment to Heal Your Life*

- *Marvelous Messages from Your Childhood: Thirteen Traits that Reveal Your Hidden Potential and Empower You to Answer the Calling of Your Heart*

- Be sure to watch for other forthcoming works in the Marvelous Messages series of books, including *Marvelous Messages from Your Ancestry* and its accompanying card deck.

View her books on Amazon here: https://amzn.to/3s837aJ

Jamie has trained with many professional practitioners, healers, and coaches including Elaine and Mark Thomas, Tom Cratsley, Donna Eden, Bill Coller, Lisa Williams, Shirley Caulkins Smith, Sharon Klingler, Sig Longren, Joey Korn, Daniel Hardt, (and many more). She is certified Reiki I. She is a minister and multi-certified graduate of Lily Dale's Fellowships of the Spirit.

In her free time, Jamie enjoys needlecrafts, making jewelry, and golf. She spends time studying spirituality, metaphysics, and parapsychology. She is a Mac geek and spends way too much time on the computer. She lives in PA and NY with her husband and a very spoiled cat. She has two grown sons.

Follow Jamie on the web at:

- **Facebook:** www.facebook.com/JamieLSaloff
- **Instagram**: www.instagram.com/jamie_saloff
- **Twitter:** http://twitter.com/JamieSaloff
- **Linkedin:** www.linkedin.com/in/jamiesaloff

What Others Are Saying About Jamie

"My session with Jamie felt like a FASCINATING journey through my body and my issues with chronic pain. She provided me with great insight as to how to move forward in the healing process, and how to "lighten my load." I seriously had one "Ah-ha" moment after another! After our session ended, I sat quietly contemplating what had been revealed to me through Jamie, and I felt totally empowered to take action in finding the balance needed to heal certain areas of my life. I highly recommend working with Jamie!"

~ Joy Phillips, OnceUponAnArchetype.com

"Jamie does something that is very wonderful. When I started talking with her I felt like I was stuck in a dark forest and did not know which way to turn. Jamie very calmly started asking me questions and making some great connections based on what I was telling her. She took me through the bushes and brambles and lead me into the light. I am now moving forward in the direction that is right for me. Thanks, Jamie, You Rock!"

~ LeeAnn Putnam

"Jamie Saloff is an amazing coach! Her insight and intuition mean she has the incredible ability to get to the heart of the matter quickly and come up with workable practical solutions just as quickly. I was struggling with a thorny personal issue and within just one hour Jamie helped me feel lighter, happier and I knew the clear path to resolve the issue. Easy as pie! If you need help sorting out some of the challenges you face—not just a person to vent to—but someone who will help you arrive at real, workable solutions, contact her today! Thanks, Jamie."

~ Denise Michaels, Las Vegas, NV, DeniseMichaels.com

I am grateful to Jamie for her intuitive listening skills and her ability to help me to understand how my body is telling where to focus attention on my life's journey. Her guidance as a medium brought phenomenal comfort to me. I applaud Jamie's skills and appreciate the knowledge, compassion, and excitement she brings to each session. She is a helper, a healer, and a conduit of messages.

~ Carolyn Hilsdon Gilles

www.ingramcontent.com/pod-product-compliance
Lightning Source LLC
Chambersburg PA
CBHW052115070526
44584CB00017B/2493